Experiments in Dreaming

Experiments in Dreaming

A Journal to Uncover Your Subconscious

Andrea Kasprzak

Art by **Oak Gallery**

CHRONICLE BOOKS
SAN FRANCISCO

ISBN 978-1-7972-0968-5

Manufactured in China.

Art by Oak Gallery (Marine Echavidre).
Design by Lizzie Vaughan.
Typeset in Raleway.

10 9 8 7 6 5 4 3 2 1

Chronicle Books LLC
680 Second Street
San Francisco, California 94107
www.chroniclebooks.com

INTENTION

TABLE OF CONTENTS

INTRODUCTION

"OUR DREAMS ARE A SECOND LIFE."
—GÉRARD DE NERVAL

Years ago, I found myself stuck.

Or at least that's the story I kept telling myself.

An insatiably curious soul, I looked for inspiration every-where—in my social media feeds, in nature, and on the shelves of the local used bookstore.

Then, I went to sleep and had the wildest dream.

In my dream, I stood behind a beautiful author with angel wings tattooed on his back. We were in an outdoor audito-rium. Everyone was talking about writing. In the next scene, I pondered the existence of supernatural forces with a famous talk show host. He asked me if I thought he was a vampire.

To anyone else in the universe, my surreal dream sequences would hold less significance than a can of pinto beans. But to me, a writer who has used dreamworlds to create narratives with meaning and direction, this dream contained exactly the message I needed to hear at that particular moment in time.

Throughout my life, dreams have served many roles. They've helped me manage the uncertainties of a career as a writer, provided space to grieve past relationships, and presented guidance on important life decisions, just to list a few. I don't rely on outside opinions to dictate meaning, but instead draw upon my own insight and vision.

Many people dismiss their dreams, but dreams have the potential to be endlessly illuminating when we simply commit to spending more time with them. After all, everyone dreams.

The average human has between three and eight dreams a night. If a person sleeps every night and lives seventy-five years, that equals about 136,875 dreams in one lifetime.

We know that dreams are the stories the brain tells during sleep, but why we dream remains elusive. Throughout time, there have been many different explanations. Ancient Egyptians believed that dreams were prophecies of what was to come. In Mesopotamia, like in Greek myth, dreams were the means through which the gods communicated with mortals. In the Romantic era, poets considered an intense dream life essential to the creative process. Maybe the reason we dream is to receive the messages our soul ignores in waking life.

Dreams, like clouds, are light and airy. We have but a limited amount of time to take note of them before they fade away forever. But instead of defaulting to standard search engine meanings for specific situations, let's continue to journey inward. Every dream has multiple meanings, various layers and levels merging and melding to create metaphors of personal experience. Only the dreamer can know with absolute certainty which interpretations hold truth.

Many dream journals are more prescriptive in nature. They approach the subject of dreaming through a purely analytical or psychological lens. But what would happen if we dared to approach our dream life with the inventiveness and intuition of an artist?

This journal is a place for you to do just that. Through conceptual instructions, journaling prompts, and dream stories, you're invited to dig deeper into your dreamworlds and report back with your findings. Think of it as part guided journal, part activity book for the time you spend dreaming.

Choosing to be an observer, to reflect and make our own meaning out of symbols and sequences, empowers us to use dreaming as a valuable tool for self-discovery. In doing so, you will discover truths that may be elusive to you in waking life—your greatest desires, your biggest fears, your deepest traumas. The simple commitment to remain open to the power of dreams is enough to begin the journey.

This journal is intended to be invitational. On these pages, I outline and provide prompts for ten different types of dreams and the benefits of each. As you begin recording your dreams, it will become easier to categorize them. Allow these categories to serve as a loose framework for exploring your dream messages. Perhaps a prompt will inspire an entirely new dream experiment that you wish to try. Or you may find that you have your own additions or edits to the prompts presented here. The nature of dreaming is fluid, as are the concepts presented in this journal.

Intuition is our own inner compass. We are all intuitive, yet have been conditioned to believe the answers are found outside ourselves. The more you learn to trust your intuition and begin to create your own meanings, the more you will discover how to give expression to the images, emotions, and energies of your dreams. You will be guided on how to analyze, intuit, evaluate, explore, and push the boundaries of your dreams.

It is an art in itself to record and understand our dreams. The most important guideline is to approach your dream recording with a childlike sense of wonder. Trust your initial feelings. Ask questions. When the mind is playful and open, there is a much greater likelihood of unlocking wisdom that could forever impact the direction of your life.

Emily Brontë once wrote that dreams had the power to color and alter the mind. Like Brontë, I too believe in the magic of dreams, in the dreamer's ability to venture into uncharted inner worlds and bring back the sensations and visions experienced in this mystical terrain. Allow this journal to guide you into the realm of the soul, and feel free to invent and add your own ideas along the way.

SEVEN TIPS FOR BETTER DREAM RECALL

1

Set an intention to remember your dreams.
The simple decision to be interested in your dreams
is the single most important step for dream recall.

2

**Before sleeping, mentally incubate
your intention to remember your dreams.**
You may also repeat an affirmation to yourself
before going to bed: "I will remember my dreams tonight."

3

Find a dream buddy.
When we surround ourselves with like-minded
people who share our interests and values, it is easier
to remain committed to our practices. Even if you do
not regularly share dreams with your dream buddy,
this person can help hold you accountable.

4

Decide how you're going to record your dreams.
Will you speak your dreams into a voice memo? Or will you
write them down in a notebook kept near your bed? Having
a plan for how you will record dreams can help with recall.

5

Title and record your dreams as soon as you wake up.
Dreams disappear quickly—if we don't commit
to jotting them down while they are fresh in our
minds, they tend to escape.

6

Establish proper sleep hygiene.
A healthy sleeping routine means going to bed around the
same time each night and waking up around the same time
each morning. Limit mindless technology use before bed.
Instead, repeat your intention, replay your day, or visualize
a calming scene. If you can wake up without the use of an
alarm clock, that can also help with dream recall.

7

Take your B vitamins.
Studies have shown that taking vitamin B_6 before
sleep may help with dream recall. These vitamins
appear to be important in the chemistry of dream
memory and can also reduce stress.

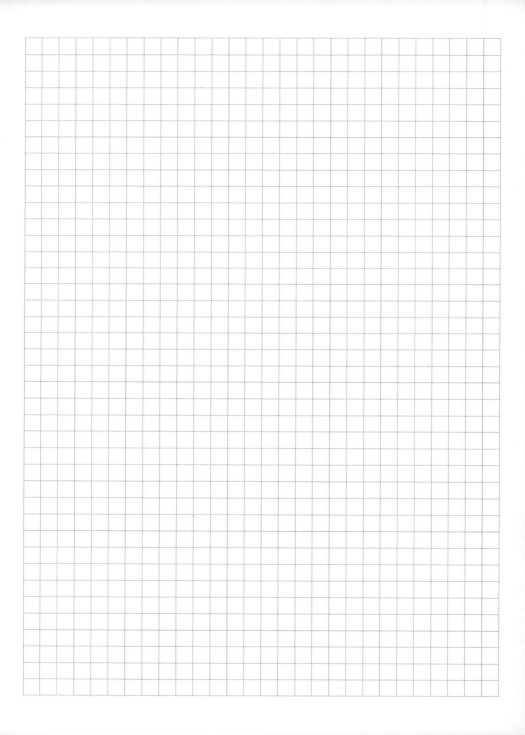

I

THE CREATIVE DREAM

USING DREAMS TO UNLEASH ARTISTIC VISION

A few years ago, I watched a recent adaptation of *Alice in Wonderland*, allowing the imaginary characters and surreal landscape to swirl around in my consciousness right before going to sleep. That night, I dreamt a vivid image of three women with glitter smeared across their eyelids. They opened their mouths to reveal fangs. The women were beautiful, yet demonic, the actual dreamworld manifestation of characters I had been secretly researching and plotting for the past five years. Before, these characters were only real to me in mood boards and early drafts of the story. But seeing them in my dream gave me a jolt of inspiration.

I woke up with renewed faith in my idea. If it could be real in my dream, it could be real in waking life.

That creative dreams have power should come as no surprise; artistic vision often appears when we release our illusion of control over a creative project. The emotional, unexpected, and vivid nature of dreams makes them an ideal and authentic source for ideas. In the dream state, our brain is active in a more visual and intuitive way. By making contact with the subconscious, we have the ability to bring exciting new ideas to life.

For centuries, artists have treated their dreams as portals to hidden worlds. In Japan, Ukiyo-e artists took many influences from ethereal themes, such as folklore, mythology, and dreamscapes. In European literature, the Romantics believed that dreams represented the artist's highest creative potential. Symbolists saw dreams as a means of deciphering reality and exploring the mysteries of existence. Surrealists combined this visionary impulse with a focus on the subconscious, suggesting that seemingly irrational content could contain significant meaning.

Today, artists still continue to derive insight from dreamy realms. Dreams are so influential to creativity that the International Association for the Study of Dreams even holds an annual juried show of dream art.

Although we cannot force a creative dream vision to occur, the media that we choose to consume before bedtime can have a positive influence on our creativity and dreamworlds. Even the simple awareness of creative dreams can open you up to experiencing them. The beauty of dreams is that they are always surprising. The following prompts will help guide you through the process of mining your dreams for their creative potential. Be receptive to whatever comes up.

LIST

For one week, set an intention that you will be mindful of what appears to you in your dreams. In the following pages list any vivid images, symbols, or sequences that you remember from your dreams. Leave space following each entry for analyzing. The following week, return to each listed item. Ask yourself: What does this entry mean to me? What fascinates me about this item? Do any of these entries excite me enough to explore them in greater detail? Do I have recurring images?

THE CREATIVE DREAM

INFLUENCES

The media that we choose to consume before bed has the power to influence our dreams. Make a list of ten films or television shows that you found to be inspirational when you were a child. Choose one of the titles on the list and, before bed, watch it and set an intention that you will remember your dreams that night. Keep this journal close to your bed along with a pen, and jot down freely everything that you remember from the dream. Do not worry about proper sentences. Feel free to list items, draw pictures, or report your findings in another way that makes sense to you. Repeat this exercise with as many of the films and television shows as you'd like. Do you notice any patterns? Are there any recurring images? How do you feel the media influenced your dreams?

Set an intention before bed that you will remember your dreams. When you wake, write your dream in the present tense. Then, go down the list of objects and characters from the dream and take turns becoming each one. For example, if your dream included a spider, relive the dream in your waking life as the spider. To do this, close your eyes and imagine the scene that you dreamt. By imagining yourself as one of the objects in your dream, you will intuitively discover the significance and message that object offers. This information can be immensely valuable when creating art because it opens us up to the full spectrum of the self, not just the comfortable or curated projection that defines us in waking life. Often, the ego prevents us from exploring repressed or dormant projections of the self. In dreaming, we have the freedom to acknowledge these projections. What does each object say to you? What past memories or associations do you have with this object? What is the first thing that comes to mind when you think of this object? Write or draw the messages from this object in the following pages.

MEDIUM

Often artists can become blocked when they're too focused on their chosen medium. When we mix it up, our ideas have space to flow more freely. Set an intention to remember your dreams. When you wake, write down the dream so the details are fresh in your mind. Now explore your dream through a creative medium that you don't usually engage with. If you're a writer, try singing. If you're a dancer, write. If you're a singer, paint. This removes the pressure to control the results and allows the mind to work more intuitively. Pay attention to any symbols that come up or images that stand out. Give yourself full permission for creative release.

II.

THE ORACLE DREAM

USING DREAMS TO FIND GUIDANCE

Earlier this year, I parted ways with a literary agent and was feeling genuinely flustered about the writing life in general. One night, I dreamt that I was messaging online with another author. This author was someone whose fantastical works had found great success. I was telling this author about my ideas, and we were messaging back and forth at a frenetic pace. I woke up and felt incredible excitement. The joy stayed with me all day. I have often used joy as a compass for what action to take next. To me, this author represented ambition and authenticity. When I was communicating with that reflection, I felt inspired and alive. The connection I experienced in my dream was electric enough to be felt in my waking life the next day. This confirmed my desire to reconnect to those qualities. Although I could have watched countless YouTube videos for inspiration, this dream felt like it was relaying important guidance from my soul.

Dreams provide more powerful guidance than any intuitive healer or pack of tarot cards, if we choose to listen. They remind us that we never have to go outside of ourselves when we are looking for answers to life's questions.

Our dreams are imbued with the knowledge of everything that is individual and special to us—our memories, our emotions, our formative media, our past experiences. When we learn how to trust our own interpretations of our dreams in response to our most troubling questions, we can discover the clarity we are seeking.

In ancient Egyptian times, the dreamworld was often viewed as prophetic. Egyptians believed the dreamworld existed as a sort of liminal space, a bridge between the world of the living and the other side. Dreams were believed to be messages from these spiritual entities. The ancient Egyptians believed so deeply in the power of dreams to foretell the future and provide advice that they held rituals to incubate their dreams. Dream incubation was a popular practice across Egyptian, Mesopotamian, and Greek civilizations. The process was similar: A person would visit a temple or holy space, offer a payment to the keepers of the temple, consume specific foods and/or fast, and then sleep overnight in the sacred space.

We too can learn how to interpret the images we receive in dreams for guidance. It can be as simple as setting an intention or asking a question. When using dreams as oracles, take into account the emotional impact of each dream. The following prompts are designed to help you become aware of your feelings about each dream and teach you how to use that information for guidance.

Before you go to sleep, write about any people, problems, or situations that are occupying space in your mind. Do not worry about how you write. If it helps to make lists, make lists. If you prefer to draw, doodle a picture. After you wake up each morning, stay in bed. If you sleep with a partner or a pet, refrain from engaging and also from using your phone. Keep your eyes closed and replay the dream, concentrating on any emotions that emerge during this time of reflection. When you record your dream in the following pages, be mindful to include feelings brought up by objects or events in the dream. What are the repetitive feelings you experienced in your dreams this week? Do the feelings surprise you or reinforce what you already know? Are you able or inspired to take action in a specific direction because of the dream? Do you enjoy these feelings or hope to change them? Do you feel compelled to make changes in your waking life because of them?

Before you go to sleep, write a question over and over, at least ten times. You may also write about any frustrations, concerns, or issues you are hoping to work out while dreaming. Set an intention to remember your dreams. When you wake, write out the dream. Now, return to your original question. Pick a specific symbol or object from the dream, and fill the pages with memories, ideas, thoughts, inspirations, or experiences about it. Let go of the desire to be logical and allow yourself to flow freely with your original thoughts. Go wherever your mind takes you. Give yourself permission to jump from idea to idea, to be abstract. Take space away from what you wrote but keep the ideas in your mind as you move throughout the day. This creates a new mental framework in your mind. Your brain will naturally begin to process the information received in its own unique way. As you move throughout the day, pay attention to anything that "lights you up"—a tweet, a book, a sign, a song, a movie, a phrase, an animal. Record this information in the following space. What do you notice? Is there any theme or connective pattern? Are you able to see your question in a new light? What sense are you able to make out of what you saw and dreamt?

The verb *consider* comes from the Latin for "contemplate." Embedded in the word consider is *sid*, the Latin root for "star." This word originally applied to the act of stargazing and experiencing the mystical qualities of the cosmos. Often, we do not give time to simply consider in our modern world. We are quick to jump on social media or plug the question into Google. Begin this exercise by setting an intention to remember your dreams and letting go of any expectations of how and what the dream message will be. In the morning, spend several minutes in bed recalling your dreams. It is OK if you only remember fragments or scenes. Write your dream fragments down in a notebook. Do not look up meanings or consult an outside source. Instead, sit in contemplation. Messages often come to us when we are in a relaxed state. Block out a short period of uninterrupted time to sit and allow meanings, messages, and thoughts to come to you. Do not judge or rationalize whatever comes up. Detach yourself from expectation, distraction, or drama. Jot down every thought, idea, image, or inspiration. Return to your notes later in the week, keeping your original intention in mind. What messages are you able to decipher from your notes? What guidance does your dream have to offer?

When we first begin to work with dreams, it can be very strange because we are teaching ourselves a new language—the language of our dreams, of our subconscious. We are also discovering what particular meaning we assign to common objects, places, and people. When you read a story or watch a movie, you realize that each character makes sense of their surroundings in a unique way. Every person has a unique lens on life. For example, the world of Oz means something much different to Glinda than it does to Dorothy. To practice this exercise, set an intention to remember your dreams. Each morning, write down whatever you recall about your dreams. Then, break it down one step further. Imagine you are describing your dreams to a creature who has no idea what any of these objects or people mean. For example, perhaps you write: "A perfume bottle sat on the shelf." You would need to break this idea down by asking yourself: What is a perfume bottle? What is a shelf? Pay attention to what you write and whether any specific memories or experiences come up. These often illuminate how we truly feel about the subject. If a particular person appears in your dream, ask: What does this person represent to me? What is the first word I think of when I hear this person's name? What qualities about them do I like or dislike? Freely jot down any associations you have with places, objects, people, or any other element of your dream. The more awareness we have for our own perspectives, the more valuable our dream fragments become to us.

III

THE INSPIRATIONAL DREAM

USING DREAMS TO MOVE PAST FEAR

Many years ago, I began to crave more freedom. At the time, I was working seven days a week at a popular women's lifestyle site and barely had time left over for a personal life, let alone the space necessary to work on my own writing, interests, and identity outside of the one dictated to me by my job. When the company folded, I found myself at a crossroads: work to maintain my comfortable, glossy lifestyle by seeking out another similar opportunity or follow my heart, leave the city and my friends behind, and reconnect to my passions. At first, the decision was scary. I had worked hard to achieve this so-called aspirational lifestyle I once thought I desired. The creative path was so uncertain. I would have to start over from scratch.

After a month of living in limbo between the two paths, I had the most beautiful dream. In the dream, I was traveling on an escalator up to a grand stage. Backstage, I found my maternal grandmother and her neighbor Marge. I remember my grandmother's skin was glowing. She truly appeared lit from within. She told me not to be afraid, to step out onto the stage, and to speak and write my own lines. I woke up so emotional from her words that I had tears in my eyes. The dream stayed with me all morning. I was so moved that I later recounted the dream to my mom on my afternoon walk through Golden Gate Park in San Francisco. "I wasn't going to tell you this," my mom told me. "But last night I asked Grandma to give you guidance and inspiration."

Like a deep affirming breath, the word *inspire* motivates another to take creative action. Often, inspiration is in reference to a creative passion, such as literature or music, but it doesn't have to be limited to artistic pursuits. Sometimes we need inspiration to believe in love again, get through a particularly challenging time, or make a big decision. Often, we look to others to be a source of inspiration, but this can backfire. We may become envious. We may compare ourselves to that person and feel discouraged about our progress. We may drain our family, friends, and romantic partners. We tend to overlook the idea that sometimes the most useful inspiration is available to us free of charge: our dreamworlds.

Throughout history, dreamworlds have inspired everyone from scientists to tech entrepreneurs to authors. When we take our dream messages seriously, avoid outside interference, and play around with possibilities, we gain inspiration that is tailor-made for us. Only scientist Friedrich August Kekule von Stradonitz's mind could have cracked the molecular structure of benzene by dreaming of snakes. Only N. K. Jemisin's mind could have turned a surreal dream about a volcanic cone into a bestselling book. Only Larry Page's mind could have spun an anxiety-fueled dream about data into the creation of Google. The truth is, we're all given the gift of inspiration through our dreams. It's up to us to use our unique way of interpreting to discover the message that is meant specifically for us.

The following prompts are designed to help you mine your dreams for inspiration.

We often seek inspiration from outside sources—from wise loved ones, trusted mentors, or those who have succeeded in accomplishing what we wish to accomplish. But instead of going direct to the source, this exercise invites you to summon their wisdom through your own subconscious. Set an intention to remember your dreams. Before sleep, either speak a request or write one to the person you admire. This person can be living or deceased. If it helps to look at this person's photo as you make your request, do so. Concentrate on their image as you are falling asleep. In the morning, record your dream fragments. Did this person appear in your dreams? If not, what or who did? How do these images relate to your understanding of this person? Allow yourself to write and process freely. Do not censor yourself or worry about complete sentences. Jot down ideas as they come to mind. Remember, no one will read this but you. The more you practice freewriting—the act of writing without any preconceived expectations or structure and without judging what you write—the easier it becomes.

SURRENDER

Sometimes, the more we fixate on a particular outcome, the further we push it away from us. Inspiration is no different. So rarely do we find it when we are looking for it, but we often do when we release control and are able to let go. In the morning, empty your mind out on paper. Write down your fears, blocks, anything occupying space in your current reality. Imagine your mind empty now that these concerns have been safely transferred to the page. Make a commitment to stay off social media for as long as you can. When you feel yourself going back into search or control mode, plug yourself back into your current reality. Do a simple chore. Take a walk. Drink a cup of tea. Fold laundry. Focus on tasks that you can complete in that moment, and let go completely of all desired outcomes, worries, and expectations. Record your dreams after practicing the art of surrender for a full day. Do they become clearer or more vivid? Do any messages come through? Do you notice any differences in your dreams?

SHARE

This is an exercise that involves a partner. Be careful about whom you decide to share your dream with. Is this person open-minded? It is important to feel safe, as dream sharing can be a vulnerable practice. Ask if you may share a dream, and tell your partner that you would love to hear their interpretation of the dream. Ask this person to respond to your dream fragments as if it were their dream. Instruct them to preface their responses with the words "If it were my dream . . ." and listen closely as they tell you their thoughts. Now, write what they said. Sit in consideration, paying close attention to see whether their ideas spark anything inside of you. What immediately comes to mind? What do their words mean to you? It's OK if nothing flows at first. Be patient with yourself during this process. In the following space, freewrite all your incoming thoughts and ideas based on their interpretation.

SILENCE

Spend an entire day in silence. Do not watch any TV or movies. Do not engage with social media. Do not speak to anyone. Limit text messages and electronic communication. If this is impossible because of your family or work, restrict yourself as best you can. Spend as much time as possible without using language. Ask others in your space to communicate only their most important requests. The more space we free up in our external and internal worlds, the more room we make for new inspirational ideas to flow through. Often, we become so overwhelmed following, commenting on, and digitally participating in others' lives that we don't have the space to hear our own intuitive wisdom. Or we speak mindlessly throughout our days, allowing our speech to become dominated by gossip, complaints, or limiting thoughts lacking purpose or value. By quieting ourselves and the world around us, we can easily access the beautiful state of flow required for inspirational wisdom to channel through us. Set an intention to remember your dreams. What ideas or insights come through? Do you notice a clarity in your dreams after observing silence in your waking life?

IV.

THE ILLUMINATING DREAM

USING DREAMS TO UNDERSTAND DAILY LIFE

Earlier this year, I became flooded with self-doubt. I found myself overwhelmed by social media and desperate to sell work, yet not really trusting or tapping into my intuition. I focused more on outcome than on imagination. I was burning out.

Around this time, I began to have dreams costarring my closest friend from my early twenties. In the dreams, we went on many adventures. She and I attended film festivals on East Coast islands. We ran around New York City. We starred in an HBO series. Other times, the dreams would be simple: We ate pizza together. As I journaled, I came to realize this particular person represented a time in my life when any-thing seemed possible. Our days together were often spent in bookstores dreaming up new ideas about everything— our wardrobes, articles for the magazine where we worked, and beyond.

When I contrasted this personality against my current daily life, I noticed a disconnect. Now, too focused on stability and feeling limited by past experiences, I had lost some of the wildness and joy required to access that freewheeling state of infinite inspiration. As I continued to work with the dreams, I realized my ability to access this state was not dependent on a particular person or a time in history, but rather on my behavior. I couldn't go back to those days, but I could integrate ideas and feelings significant from that particular time period into my current reality.

To do this, I rekindled my love of vintage clothing. I resumed a creative project and used fashion to form a story line in my work, just like my friend and I had done while working at the magazine. I allowed myself to write intentions again. Soon after I began practicing these behaviors, the dreams with my friend stopped. The message from my subconscious had been received.

When we learn to take our dreams seriously, we can easily notice and apply the messages that our subconscious is sending us. In doing so, we enter into a relationship with our psyche that helps us gain greater awareness and understanding of ourselves. Our dreams go much deeper than what we have access to on the daily. Even when we're actively reflecting, we may censor and restrict ourselves. Our minds rush to control the situation. We may attach to a particular emotion or identity instead of allowing ourselves permission to be truly fluid, to listen and observe whatever comes. When we're dreaming, we have access to a rich inner life: people from our past and present, strong emotions, memorable scenes. And when we learn to successfully infuse the two by integrating the messages of our dreamworlds into our waking life, the subconscious doesn't have to be quite as expressive.

The following prompts will teach you how to use your dream activity to mirror and reflect your current reality and illuminate the hidden truths that are unavailable to us in our conscious state.

NIGHT AND DAY

Before going to sleep, write three to five quick sentences about what is going on in your life. You may write about your day, current challenges, people you spoke with, where you went, or what you accomplished that day. Set an intention to remember your dreams. When you wake, write another paragraph listing any dream fragments that you recall. Do this for one entire week. Go back and reread your stories about your day and the dream fragments. Do you notice any themes or repeating patterns? Set aside a block of time to freewrite about your findings in the following space.

Set an intention to remember your dreams. For one week, keep a list of every person who appears in your dreams. Do not worry about recalling why or what happens in the dream. Instead, focus only on the people. At the end of the week, jot down three to five qualities of each person who appeared in your dreams. Is there any overlap? How do those qualities reflect you, the dreamer? Are they qualities that *you* wish to express? Are they qualities that you once expressed? Are they qualities that you like or dislike about yourself? Can you integrate any qualities of these people into your current reality? In the following space, freewrite about any ideas or thoughts that come up.

FEELINGS

Set an intention to remember your dreams. For one week,
focus on the feelings you experience both during your dreams
and when you wake up. Keep a record of these feelings in
the following space, along with a short paragraph reflecting
on how you are feeling each day in your conscious life. What
do you notice after a week of observing your subconscious
feelings? Do you feel happy, excited, blissed out, terrified,
peaceful, overwhelmed? Go with the first emotion that
presents itself to you and trust it. Now, contrast these feelings
with your daily entries on your conscious life. Do these two
worlds—the subconscious and the conscious—mirror each
other? Do they reveal any new insights? Why do you think you
feel a particular way?

Bizarre dreams can be terrifying. At first, it is tempting to take them literally. Example: A death dream means someone will die. However, when we are able to devote more time to the dream, to write it out and read it back to ourselves, new meanings and interpretations make themselves known. Set an intention to remember your dreams. When you wake, write the dream in the following space. Now, reread what you wrote to yourself. What do you notice when you hear the dream again with your own voice? Allow meaning to arrive on its own time; don't try to rush it. Jot down any observations, reflections, or insights that make themselves available to you.

V.

THE EXPERIMENTAL DREAM

USING DREAMS TO PLAY AND DISCOVER

The scent of jasmine is magical to me. The fragrance transports me to when I first moved to San Francisco, a time of full moon walks in the Lower Haight and misty-cool nights when the air smelled like flowers and it truly felt as if anything was possible. I can't ever return to those early San Francisco adventures in my waking life, but I wondered if I could somehow revisit the feelings in my dreams.

Before sleep, I applied a jasmine-scented body oil. That night, I dreamt that I was on a big ship with various staff of a literary nonprofit I am involved with. In the dream, we were all fishing. I cast my pole out into the ocean and caught a massive emerald green trout.

When I woke up and noted the dream, I realized that "fishing" is still one of my favorite parts of the creative process. As a writer, I'm constantly querying, pitching, and plotting, casting ideas out into the great big sea with no real promise that anything will ever go anywhere beyond my own imagination. As frustrating as this process is at times, it is also exciting. I can't say for certain whether it was the scent of a night-blooming flower that created this dream, but it makes for an interesting case to continue in my dream experiments.

Salvador Dalí was one of the great dream experimenters. He really believed in the power of his dreams and often used many different systems of dream control in his artistic methods. One of his most famous is his idea of "slumber with a key." This practice prescribes a very brief micro nap in which the dreamer holds a heavy key over a plate placed upside down on the floor. The idea is that when the dreamer falls asleep, the key will drop, and the noise will be enough to startle the dreamer awake. This allows the dreamer to enter the hypnagogic state, where the mind is fluid and able to allow creative connections to form, connections that may not otherwise be realized in waking life.

Scents also have the power to unlock our subconscious minds. Our sense of smell is one of the most primal and mysterious of all the senses. In 1865, French scholar Louis-Ferdinand Alfred Maury explored its link to dreams by instructing his assistant to put cologne under his nose while he was asleep. On awakening, he reported that he had dreamt he was in Cairo, in the workshop of Giovanni Maria Farina, the perfumer who invented cologne. Many experts believe it is possible we experience smells in our dreams that do not exist in our waking life.

Experimental dreams open us up to the thrilling possibility of discovering something new. The following prompts play with ideas of scent, decor, and micro napping. They are designed to be used as a jumping-off point for continued experimentation. Feel free to put your ideas into play if you are so inspired.

SMELL

Studies have shown that olfactory stimuli can influence our dreams, but not necessarily in a literal way. For example, you won't dream of a rosebush simply because you catch a whiff of the fragrance before falling asleep. Instead, studies have found that it is our emotional relationship with a particular scent that impacts our dreams. For one week, experiment with various scents before falling asleep. What scent reminds you of a first love? What scent kindles a beloved childhood memory? What scent reminds you of a happy time? Make a list of various perfumes or fragrances that hold particular memories for you. Before going to sleep, spend a minute inhaling that particular fragrance. In the morning, record your dream experiences. What do you notice?

CHEESE

Can certain foods influence your ability to dream? Do certain foods cause nightmares? All cheeses contain an amino acid called tryptophan, which is helpful in normalizing sleep and reducing stress levels. A 2005 study conducted by the British Cheese Board found that subjects who ate Cheddar dreamt more about celebrities while people who ate blue cheese experienced very odd dreams. Red Leicester inspired nostalgic dreams. Cheshire provided the best sleep. Come to your own cheese dream conclusions. For a week, keep a cheese dream record. Each night, consume a different type of cheese before bed. Report your findings.

HYPNAGOGIA

The experience between wakefulness and sleep is called *hypnagogia*. This is what Dalí experimented with during his famous "slumber with a key" exercises. In hypnagogia, you're floating in a liminal space: your mind sliding into sleep, but your awareness still lingering in the waking world. You may feel like you're bobbing, floating, flying, or falling. To try this for yourself, have a pen and paper ready in order to record your notes. Pick a small, heavy object to hold. You could try a key, a spoon, or a heavy coin. Hold it loosely. Drape your arm over the edge of your bed and place a hard plate directly below. As soon as you fall asleep, your body will relax. You'll drop the object, becoming conscious enough to jot down your visions. The more you practice, the better you'll become at this technique.

DREAM ALTAR

The items we look at before we fall asleep can influence our dreams. Practice experimenting with your dreams by creating a dream altar on your bedside table. Decorate the space according to your specific dream intention. For example, if you wish to dream about flying, tape an image of a person flying along with a bird's feather. If you wish to dream about a loved one who has since passed, tape the person's photo up along with any memorable items, belongings, or trinkets that remind you of that person. If you are an artist looking for ideas, try a blank canvas or images you've clipped that reflect the project's mood and vision. What happened in your dream that night? Record your findings.

VI

THE UNCOMFORTABLE DREAM

USING DREAMS TO WORK THROUGH FEAR

During a transitional phase, I began to dream about all of my former selves. In the dreams, I would be performing the tasks of previous jobs, except wherever I went, no one had heard of me. I tried to explain myself, but I was still being treated like a phantom.

When I reflected on the dream, the message felt obvious to me: I was releasing my former selves as I continued to hone and tap into my truest voice. It felt easier to return to what I knew versus walking forward into the unknown. But by listening to the dream, I could take the power back for myself. I recognized my triggers and then retrained myself to continue moving in a direction aligned with my soul. With awareness, the dream didn't feel so scary anymore. Instead of allowing an uncomfortable dream to cloud my mood and behavior for the entire day, I could instead take action by working on new writing projects.

The uncomfortable dream, better known as a nightmare, is a familiar experience for most people. The *Diagnostic and*

Statistical Manual of Mental Disorders estimates that about 6 percent of adults have at least one nightmare per month. Nightmares are often triggered by feelings of helplessness and vulnerability. We may not want to look too closely at a bad dream, preferring instead to move on and try to forget it. But like any other type of dream, a nightmare often deals with some aspect of ourselves we do not want to confront. In order to truly process the dream, we must suspend judgment. There is no such thing as a "bad dream." In fact, nightmares are potentially the most valuable because they force us to pay attention. What is remembered is worth remembering because it contains useful information. All dreams come to tell us something we do not already know.

The following prompts invite you to take a closer look at your most uncomfortable dreams. They will teach you not to be afraid of uncomfortable dreams but rather to be curious about them. What are these dreams trying to tell you? And more importantly, will you listen?

Make a list of your most problematic dreams. You may write
the dreams down in list form, or you may detail them in scenes.
What emotion did the dream sequence make you feel? Why do
you think it was so disturbing for you? Allow yourself permission
to feel and process that emotion. When we choose to expose
ourselves to the emotion instead of trying to repress it, we are
able to receive the message from our subconscious.

Write or draw the story of your dream in the following space. What emotions did you feel in the dream? Why? If you had the opportunity to rescript your dream with a more pleasurable ending (like a scene in a movie), how would the dream play out? Now, write or draw a new ending for your dream.

Program yourself for more pleasant dreams. Make a list of films,
TV shows, music, and stories that are aesthetically pleasant
or soothing to you. Many people return to childhood for this
exercise. Limit your exposure to hard news, social media, and
excessively violent or emotionally intense subject matter.
Instead, watch, listen to, or think about one of the items on your
list. How does focusing on comforting images or sounds before
bed impact your dreams? Do you notice any changes?

VII.
THE INTERPERSONAL DREAM

USING DREAMS TO COMMUNICATE AND RELATE

"Do you believe that we can share dreams?" asked Olivia, a new writer friend with an interest in mysticism. We were sitting outside in the back garden of a cafe in San Francisco's Haight-Ashbury neighborhood.

I recalled a couple of experiments a friend and I had conducted the year before. My friend was interviewing me for a project on synchronicities when I came up with an idea to see whether we could exchange messages with each other in our dreams. I thought to ask her because she is extremely open-minded and responsive to abstract ideas and esoteric concepts. That night before bed, I set an intention to communicate with her, and she made an appearance in my dreams.

After I shared the story with Olivia, another example of dream communication came to mind: Several years ago, my friend began regularly dreaming of her high school boyfriend. The two had not been in contact for almost a decade, but in the dreams they were together, holding hands. After hearing this, I passed along my friend's contact information to a shared connection, who forwarded the email to the man my friend was dreaming about. Turns out, he had been thinking of her as well. He phoned her immediately, inviting her out to California, where he lived. Today, they are married with a son.

Dream telepathy has a rich history that goes back thousands of years and is steeped in folklore and mythology. There have been many experiments done to test the validity of dream telepathy with varying degrees of success. One of the most iconic studies attempted to use audience participation at a six-night series of Grateful Dead concerts back in 1971. On each night, an audience of two thousand people was exposed to the target material of six slides, including an artwork, and instructed to beam the picture to two psychic sensitives working with the Dream Laboratory at Maimonides Medical Center in Brooklyn, New York. The idea was that the two psychics would receive the images in their sleep. The results: One dreamer, Felicia Parise, had only one match, but the other dreamer, Malcolm Bessent, had four out of six matches, a statistically significant result.

Whether you believe in dream telepathy or not may be the most important aspect to successfully sending and receiving dream messages. You are more likely to have success with the concept if you choose to communicate with someone who is open, receptive, and accepting of your energy. For that reason, make sure your dream telepathy is consensual; confirm all parties are comfortable with this practice before proceeding. Also, like anything, approach the concept of dream telepathy with no expectations. Let go and see what happens. This is a time to suspend your logical brain and channel your artistic brain. The magic of dreams is that they are mysterious and often surprising. When we can't prove anything for certain, the chances of new discoveries are high. Paradigm-challenging experiences are perhaps most important for science because they force revolutionary change. The following prompts will open you up to the concept of interpersonal dreaming and give you a chance to practice your skills.

Find a dream buddy who is open to the idea of sharing dreams with you. It helps if this is a person you trust and are close to. One person chooses to be the sender, the other the receiver. Start with something small. Dream telepathy isn't the place for grand confessions or marriage proposals. Concentrate before bed on the message you are sending. Encourage your partner to clear their mind, either with the aid of soothing music or an easy meditation. Focus intently on your friend's face and energy. Revisit shared memories in your mind. In the morning, compare dreams. What comes up for both of you? How is the message interpreted and received?

Find a dream buddy who is open to the idea of sharing dreams with you. Set a specific sleep time and place you'll try to meet in your dreams. Before falling asleep, both participants will picture the place—either real (Paris, your childhood backyard) or imagined (Narnia, Oz)—and focus on each other. Think of shared memories and how it feels when you are together. In the morning, share your dreams. Did you see your dream buddy in your sleep? Where did you go? What messages came up?

MESSAGES

Keep a list of all the people who appear in your dreams. When
someone makes an appearance, contact that person and tell
them about your dream. Had they been thinking of you too?

See if you can inspire contact from a particular person. It helps if this person is in your life, open to your energy, and accepting of your presence. If someone has closed you out of their life, it becomes more difficult to reach them in dreams. Obviously, a celebrity who has never heard of you before is probably less likely to be receptive to you. For a week, meditate on the person you are trying to reach. What dreams come up for you? Did this person contact you in your waking life?

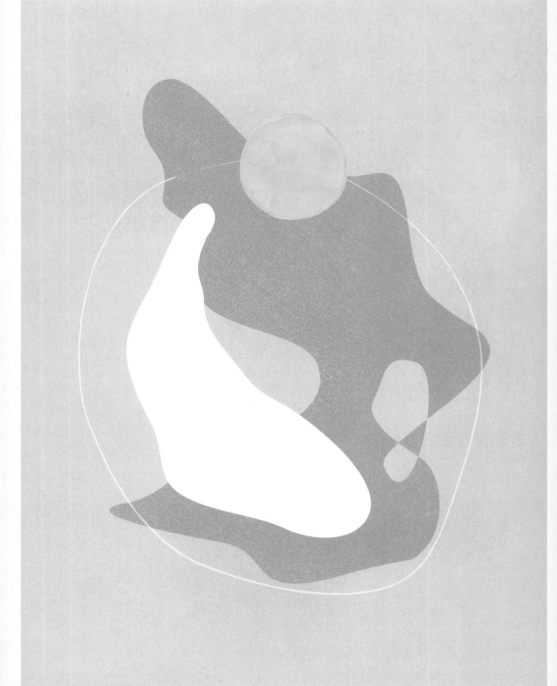

VIII.

THE SEXUAL DREAM

USING DREAMS TO EXPLORE DESIRE

I awoke one morning in a state of bliss.

In the dream, I was on my back and a male figure had his head on my chest. He and I were in a canvas tent surrounded by candles, flowers, and twinkling lights. His mouth traveled the length of my body. I leaned my head back and exhaled butterflies.

Sexual dreams are perhaps the most common, although many dream experts disagree on how they should be processed. In fact, it was a dispute about sex in dreams that drove psychologists Sigmund Freud and Carl Jung apart. Freud believed that our dreams are all about sex and repressed desires, while Jung concluded that dreams are a representation of the subconscious mind. Jung focused more on the symbolism and the imagery. In his world, dreams can have many different meanings depending on the dreamer's associations. Many dream experts today agree that when working with sexual dreams, it's best to focus on the symbolic representation. What qualities does this person represent in your current life? What emotions do you feel when their name comes up?

When I journaled about my dream, I realized that the mysterious figure and the ethereal setting symbolized freedom, beauty, and a lighthearted approach to life. It made sense to me why I would dream of this. In my waking life, my partner and I were nearing month five of being quarantined together in a condo located in noisy downtown San Francisco. Before the COVID-19 pandemic, he and I regularly planned adventures together. In fact, the dream was vaguely reminiscent of a night we spent together sleeping above the clouds on a camping trip to Big Sur. Now, with the California fires burning outside our windows and the pandemic limiting nearly every activity, it was challenging to conjure up emotions of beauty, love, and magic. The dream reminded me to prioritize this request from my soul. One afternoon, we looked for seashells on the beach. Another day, we explored a local cloud forest. I felt very inspired after our outings. It became easier for me to focus on creative projects and feel a deeper sense of peace despite the pandemic's restrictions.

Sex dreams are all about desire. What do we crave more of in our lives? What qualities are most attractive to us right now? We can also compare our sexual dreams with our current sex life to discover how we truly feel about it. What are we curious to explore with our partners?

The following prompts encourage you to work closer with your sexual dreams. They will help you become more comfortable interpreting and incorporating the wisdom from your sexual dreams into your waking life.

QUALITIES

Brainstorm a list of qualities about the person who appeared
in your sex dream. What do they represent to you? Do you like
them or hate them? Why? What qualities about this person do
you dislike? What qualities do you admire? What are some ways
you can incorporate these qualities into your own life?

LOCATION

Location in sex dreams is also interesting to explore. We often assign our own meaning to particular places. For example, Michigan, where I grew up, reminds me of safety, family, and security. Seattle, another place I lived, makes me think of solitude. This is especially interesting in sex dreams, which deal with desire. Were you having sex in a public place? In your childhood home? In your college apartment? Go back to the person you were when you lived in that space. Are you holding on to anything that you can let go of from that time? Are there aspects of yourself from that time that you need to reconnect with now? Spend time freewriting about that particular place and the memories associated with it.

SENSATIONS

Pay attention to what you notice in your body as you recall
the dream. Spend some time unplugging from devices
and technology, and replay the dream. Do you notice any
particular emotions or feelings in your body that come up?
Let your body reveal what it wants to say to you. Jot the
feelings and ideas down.

Block out a period of time to discuss your dreams with your current sexual partner. Take turns sharing recent dreams. Do not feel embarrassed or uncomfortable if your dreams feature someone else besides your partner. Sexual dreams are not meant to be taken literally. Dreaming about another person sexually does not mean that you are not attracted to your current partner. Often, these dreams force us to go deeper and reflect more on the specific characteristics, energy, and feelings of the other person. After you share your dream, invite your partner to ask you questions related to your feelings about your sex life. Is there something new you want to try? How do you feel about the frequency of your sex life? How do you feel the symbols in your dreams relate to your sex life? Now, ask your partner these questions. What do you discover?

Note: This exercise requires a lot of trust and openness; it may not be appropriate with every partner. It is important to discuss each person's stated comfort levels and boundaries before engaging in any discussion about sexual dreams.

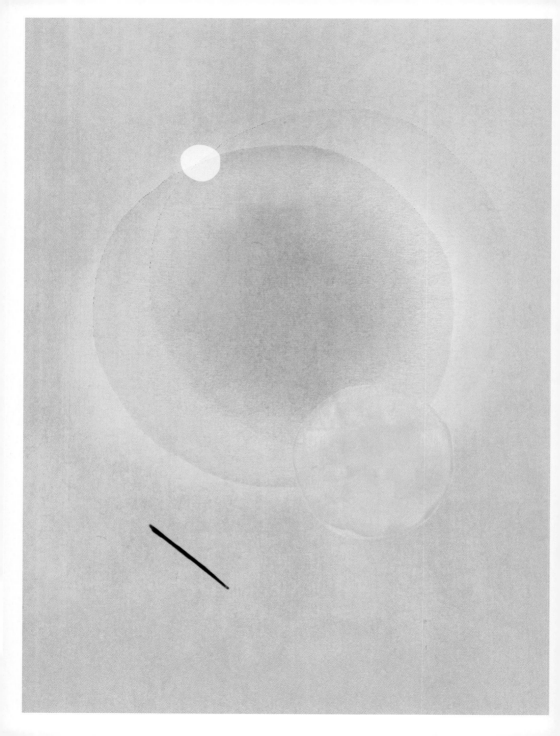

IX.

THE HEALING DREAM

USING DREAMS TO PROCESS
TRAUMA, CHANGE, AND GRIEF

When I was in my early twenties, I tried everything to erase a particular love story from my mind. I went to therapy. I moved to a small New England island where I knew only one other person. I wrote two novels. But it was only years later, when I closed my eyes one night and had a vivid dream, that I fully and finally allowed myself to let go of my suffering.

In the dream, I was on a golf course. The man I thought I was in love with was in the same black shiny car he used to pick me up in every night. I watched as he stuck out his hand and waved a slow goodbye. His long, milky white fingers blurred into the sky. Although he seemed like a ghost, somehow, I knew it was him.

Then, the car window rolled up, and he drove away from my imagination forever.

I woke up and felt the strongest sense of peace. The imagination, and especially my imagination, loves to believe that every love story that doesn't lead to a rom-com-worthy ending is unfinished business. We are often more haunted by what could have happened than by what actually did.

The dream illustrated what my soul had been trying to communicate to me all along: It is OK to let go. To my surprise, the message wasn't even painful or sad. It was actually quite beautiful.

Often in waking life, we attach to harmful narratives and create emotional dramas. We then mentally replay these stories that cause us great suffering. In the dream state, however, the soul is allowed to take center stage. If we listen, we are then able to surrender and move on. Studies have shown that when we experience an emotional situation in waking life, stress chemicals are released in order to flag its importance, reminding the brain to work through the issue during sleep. In the dream state, the brain divorces emotions from memory, which allows us to process the situation in a way that is no longer so heightened or intense. This is perhaps why it's best to "sleep on it" instead of immediately reacting to conflict from a hyperemotional place. Through dreams, we may receive a new way of viewing the situation, finally find closure, or simply wake up in a more neutral state of mind.

The following prompts invite you to use dreams to process difficult situations. They invite you to write out narratives that are causing you distress and remain receptive to the messages received in dreams. They will teach you how to better understand your own language of dream symbols and create new meaning and actions for whatever troubles you.

PURGE

Before you go to sleep, freewrite everything in your mind that is upsetting you. Allow yourself to get rid of any stories, ideas, issues, or situations that plague your mind. Set an intention to remember your dreams. In the morning, write out what you dreamt. Do you see any messages in your dreams? If so, what are they?

STORYTELLING

Before sleep, write yourself a healing story. Imagine the problem is resolved. How would that story go? If this is difficult, focus your attention on any images that help you imagine a different outcome than what is currently playing out in your mind. Set an intention for your dreams to reveal any blocks or issues in your particular narrative. In the morning, write out what you dreamt. What symbols appear in your dream? What do they mean to you? Do any people appear in your dream? What do these particular people represent to you?

PLACE

Before sleep, spend several minutes incubating the visual
of a place where you feel most safe. What symbols, people,
or places represent a sense of safety to you? It could be a
childhood treehouse. It could be an imaginary world in a
storybook. It could be the park where you walk with your loved
one or children each day. Allow yourself to mentally go to this
place. In the morning, write out your dreams. What symbols or
people appear in your dream? Do you sense any messages?

MUSIC

In another room, play a song that is soothing to you on repeat.
The volume should be set low, soft enough that you can barely
hear the words but loud enough that you know it's playing. Set
an intention to remember your dreams. In the morning, write
out what you dreamt. Do you feel the music influenced your
dreams? Do any messages come through?

X.

THE RECURRING DREAM

USING DREAMS TO UNDERSTAND PATTERNS

Years ago, I had the same dream night after night. My coworkers and I were at a fancy party. We sat in high-backed pink chairs and drank champagne cocktails with wobbly bobbly berries inside. One of my colleagues took a sip and her eyes widened. She pointed at me. To my horror, I'd somehow sprouted translucent fairy wings. The wings protruded out of the back of my tulle party dress. I'd been found out. They knew. I didn't belong there.

At the time, the dream terrified me. Somehow I had formed this belief that it was impossible to cross-pollinate my different selves. I believed that they were separate and if I veered too far into one world, I would be banned from the other. It felt safer to repress the parts of myself that I had been told were strange.

When that job ended, I had nothing but time and space to explore and find acceptance for those so-called "weird" sides of myself. For the first time in a long time, I was free. I wrote stories about mermaids, supernatural powers, and the beauty of the imagination. I sat on a Hawaiian beach and read anthologies of fantasy stories. Instead of attending posh parties, I went to secret gatherings where artists juggled glow-in-the-dark balls and read poems out loud. I saw art films at a small independent theater owned by a woman who, post-viewing, gifted moviegoers a mango wrapped in a paper towel. And those recurring fairy dreams stopped entirely.

A friend once became very troubled by her recurring dream. She told me that her dreams scared her so much that she didn't want to remember them anymore. But dreams, no matter how intense or revealing they may be, are not meant to be feared. To fear a dream is to give away our power. A dream is merely a message, open for interpretation by the dreamer. We, the dreamers, have the ability to choose how we want to live our lives. As a bridge between the subconscious and conscious minds, dreams give us guidance. When you learn to speak the language of dreams, you realize that neither the dreams nor the dreamer is wrong or crazy. When we take the time to understand, we are no longer haunted. The dreams are an opportunity to receive guidance from the subconscious on how to work through patterns we continue to repeat in daily life. What changes do our dreams urge us to make? And most importantly, will we be brave enough to make them?

Recurring dreams are not always unpleasant. Many people report recurring dreams of soaring high above the sky like a bird, playing as a child, or other peaceful scenes.

The following prompts invite you to take a closer look at your recurring dreams. You will learn how to decipher your own dream language so you can create positive change in your conscious life.

PATTERNS

Write down the story of your recurring dream. Now, write out
what is happening in your life. Feel free to write about whatever
comes up for you: love, work, friends, family, or any particular
stresses you may be dealing with at this time. Now look back at
the dream. What are the first thoughts that come to mind? What
fears does the dream bring up? Why do you think you're afraid?
What changes in your waking life could you begin to make that
will put your mind at ease?

Write out the story of your recurring dream. Enter a meditative state by closing your eyes and taking some deep breaths. Make sure you are in a comfortable position. Now, enter the dream. Go up to each character in the dream and tell them the first thought that comes to mind. What do you need to say to them in order to rewrite the dream? Rewrite the story of your recurring dream using the guidance from your visualization.

SYMBOLS

Jot down any symbols that appear in your recurring dream.
You can do this in list form, if that is easier for you. Now, write
out what comes to mind when you think of that symbol. Allow
yourself freedom to go with your first initial thoughts. Let ideas
arrive in their own time. Now, write out what is happening in
your current life. How do the symbols tie in? Do you notice any
connections?

List the people and characters who appear in your recurring dream. What are the characteristics of each of these people? If they are people you don't know, what are the first words that come to mind when you think of them? How do these characteristics play into your current reality? Are they qualities you share? Or ones you desire or fear? What changes can you make to incorporate these qualities or behave in a different way? If they are qualities you have trouble accepting in yourself, allow yourself to be fully present with them. Journal freely about whatever comes up. Sit with the feeling, acknowledge it, and when you are ready, release it.

CONCLUSION

DREAMS ARE A STRANGE MAGIC

As you continue recording and reflecting on your dreams, you will learn to make your own meaning and create your own dream language. You will discover new truths about yourself and your personal narratives.

Open up to the mystical and the mysterious, and watch as your entire world becomes richer. Life will begin to unfold in seemingly supernatural, synchronistic, and serendipitous ways. You will begin to make helpful connections that previously eluded you in waking life.

Whenever we dare to go deeper, reality in turn becomes much more sublime.